**ORIGINAL KEYS** *for* **SINGERS**

# once

music from the motion picture soundtrack

T0085655

ISBN 978-1-4768-1370-7

HAL•LEONARD®
CORPORATION
7777 W. BLUEMOUND RD. P.O. BOX 13819 MILWAUKEE, WI 53213

In Australia Contact:
Hal Leonard Australia Pty. Ltd.
4 Lentara Court
Cheltenham, Victoria, 3192 Australia
Email: ausadmin@halleonard.com.au

Visit Hal Leonard Online at
www.halleonard.com

# FALLING SLOWLY

Words and Music by GLEN HANSARD
and MARKETA IRGLOVA

**Moderately slow**

I don't know you, but I want you

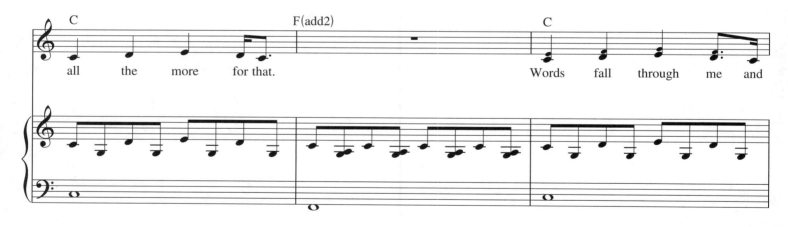

all the more for that. Words fall through me and

al - ways fool me, and I can't re - act.

Now you're gone. ___

# IF YOU WANT ME

Words and Music by
MARKETA IRGLOVA

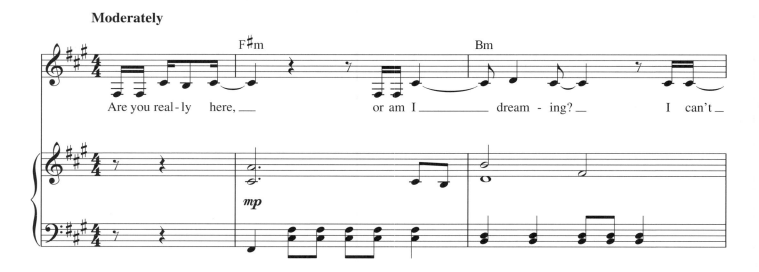

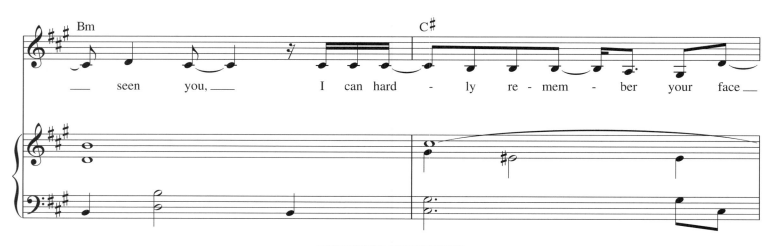

# BROKEN HEARTED HOOVER FIXER SUCKER GUY

Words and Music by
GLEN HANSARD

Moderately fast

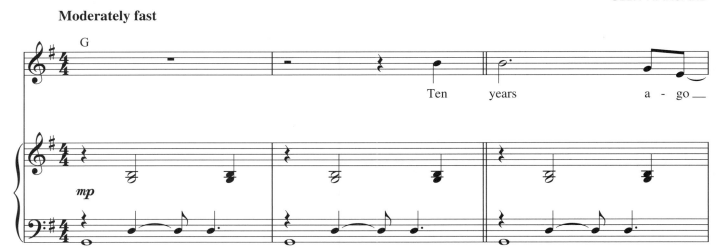

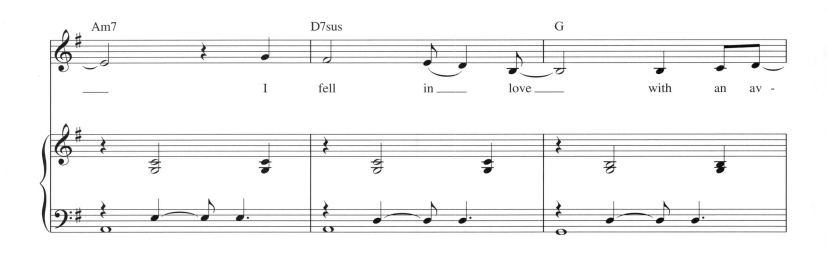

# WHEN YOUR MIND'S MADE UP

Words and Music by
GLEN HANSARD

**Moderately fast**

So _____

if you ev-er want some-thing, _
you're just like ev-'ry-one: _____

and you
when the

# LIES

Words and Music by GLEN HANSARD
and MARKETA IRGLOVA

will __ you learn? __

The

So plant the thought and

watch it grow. Wind it up and let it go.

# GOLD

Words and Music by
FERGUS O'FARRELL

**Moderately, in 1**

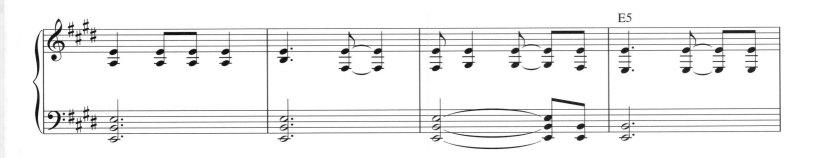

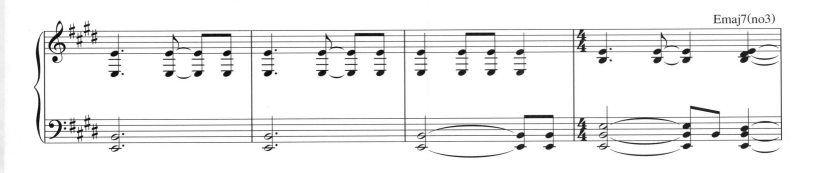

And I love her so;
if a door be closed,

I would-n't trade her for
then a row of her homes start

gold.
build - ing.

I'm
And

Hey! —

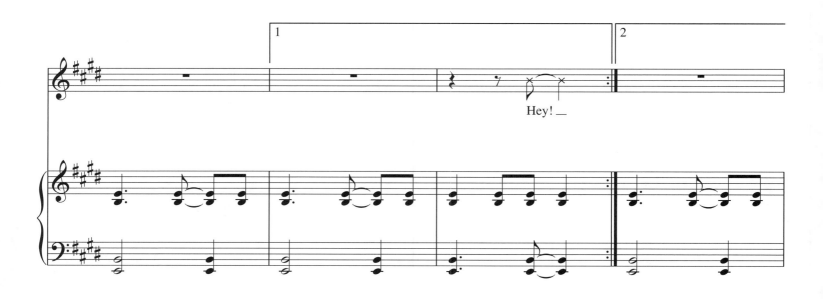

# THE HILL

Words and Music by
MARKETA IRGLOVA

**Moderately slow**

Walk- ing up the hill to- night when
please try to be pa- tient, and
Look- ing at you sleep- ing, I'm

you have closed your eyes, I
know that I'm still learn- ing. I'm
with the man I know; I'm

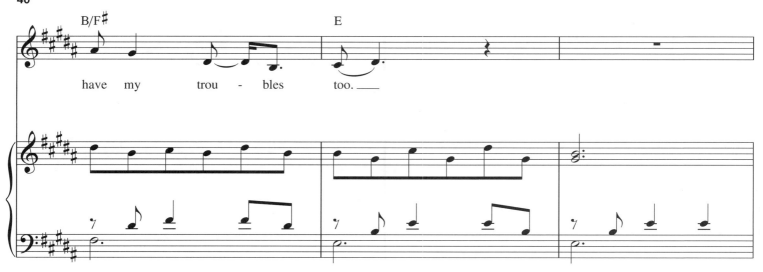

have my trou - bles too. ____

**Slightly faster**

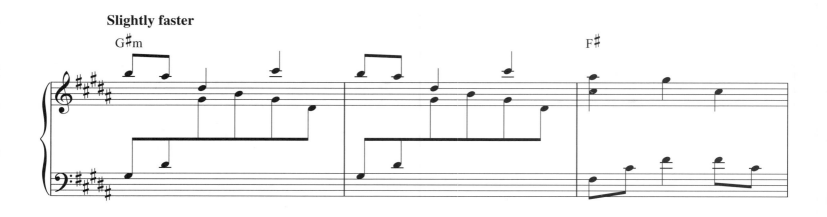

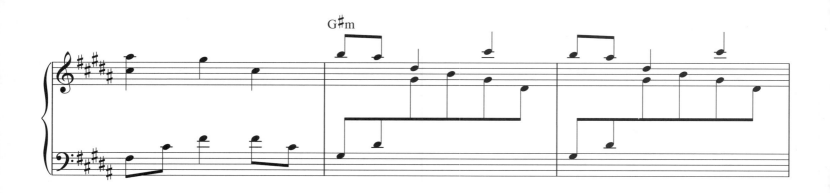

D.S. al Coda

**CODA**

# FALLEN FROM THE SKY

Words and Music by
GLEN HANSARD

**Moderately**

Emaj7

You must have fall-en from the sky.

C#m7     F#m11

You must have shat-tered on the run-way.

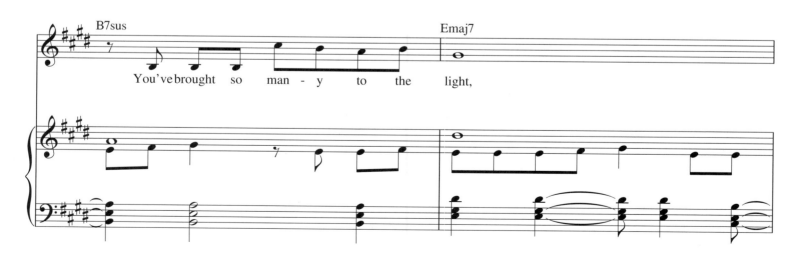

B7sus     Emaj7

You've brought so man-y to the light,

# LEAVE

Words and Music by
GLEN HANSARD

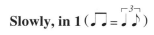

**Slowly, in 1**

"I can't wait for-ev-er,"
And I hope you feel bet-ter,
is
now

all that you said
be - fore you stood up.
that it's out.
What took you so long?

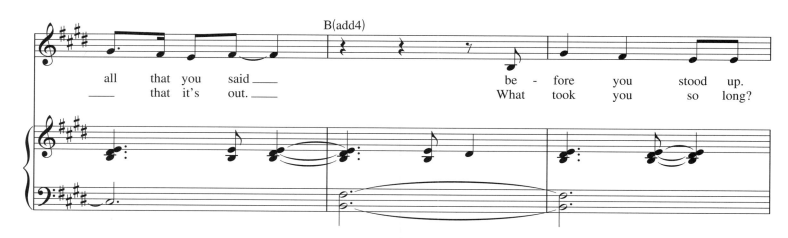

# TRYING TO PULL MYSELF AWAY

Words and Music by
GLEN HANSARD

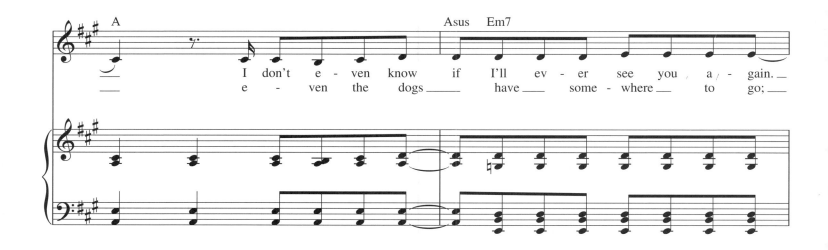

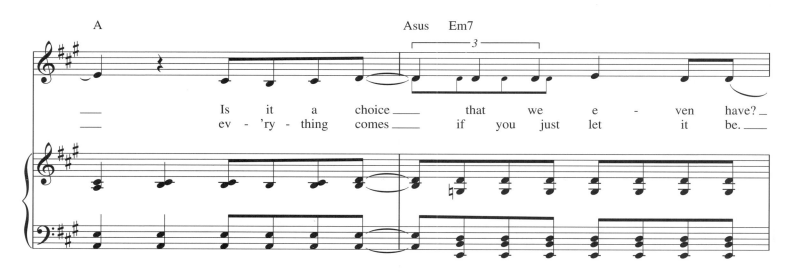

# ALL THE WAY DOWN

**Moderately slow**

You have bro-ken me ___ all ___ the way down, ___
And you have bro-ken me ___ all ___ the way down. ___

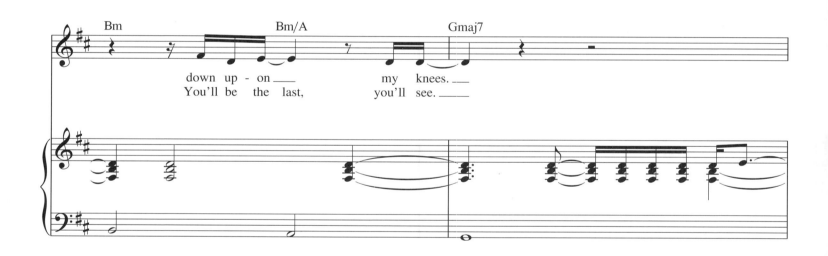

down up-on ___ my knees. ___
You'll be the last, you'll see. ___

And you have bro-ken me ___ all ___ the way now. ___
*Lead vocal ad lib.)*

the way down. ____ You'll be the last; you'll see. ____

# ONCE

Words and Music by
GLEN HANSARD

**Moderately slow, in 2**

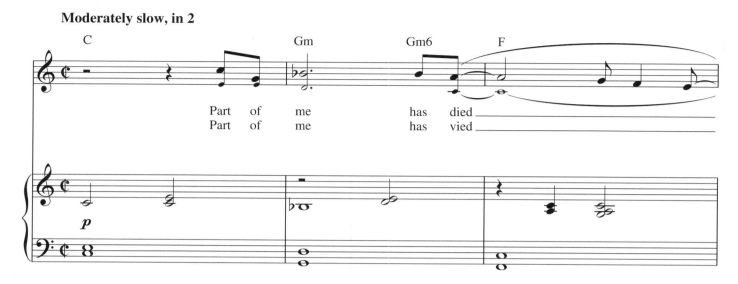

Part of me has died _____
Part of me has vied _____

and won't re - turn.
to watch it burn.

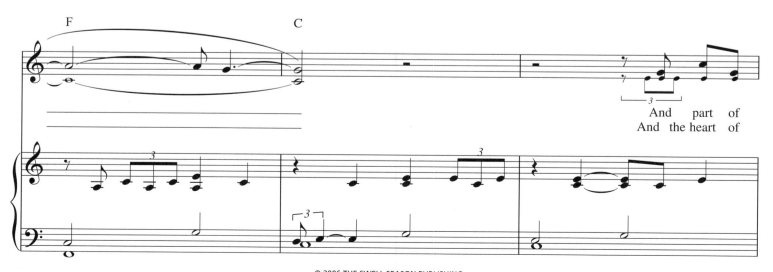

And part of
And the heart of

# SAY IT TO ME NOW

Words and Music by GLEN HANSARD,
GRAHAM DOWNEY, PAUL BRENNAN,
NOREEN O'DONNELL, COLM MACCONIOMAIRE
and DAVID ODLUM

Scratch-ing at the sur-face now;

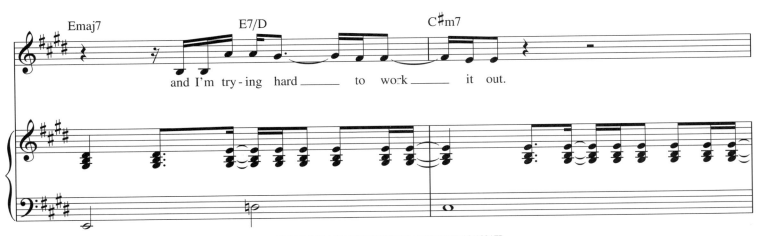

and I'm try-ing hard ____ to wo-rk ____ it out.